At the Feet of Our Elders

A Guided Journal of 30
Interview Questions for
Conversations Between Teens
and Their Elders

This Journal Belongs to

_____

Grandfa
Grandma
FAMILY
lovely
FRIENDS
MOMMY
PARENTS
Sweet
uncle
I ♥ my
family
AUNT
MOTHER
Grand
parents
DADDY
son
SISTER
home
FATHER
BROTHER
Relationship
SMILE

Elder 1:_____

Interview Date(s)

Birthday   Age

Birth City, State, Country

Mother's Name

Father's Name

Sibling's Name(s) & Ages

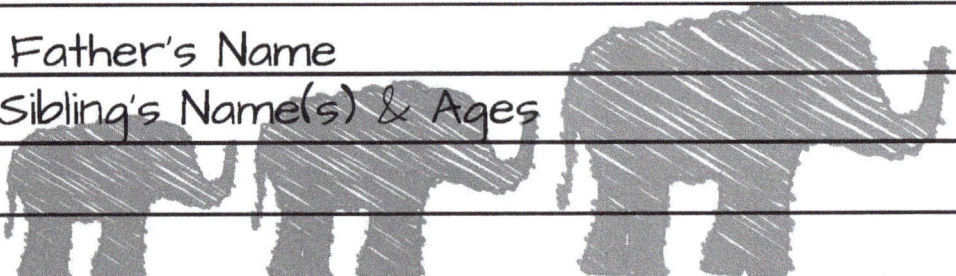

_____

_____

Elder 2_____

Interview Date(s)

                                              Age

Birth City, State, Country

Mother's Name

Father's Name

Sibling's Name(s) & Ages

Elder 3: _____

Interview Date(s)

Age

Birth City, State, Country

Mother's Name

Father's Name

Sibling's Name(s) & Ages

Elder 4: _____

Interview Date(s)

Age

Birth City, State, Country

Mother's Name

Father's Name

Sibling's Name(s) & Ages

What was school like?

*Elder 1:*_____

*Elder 2*_____

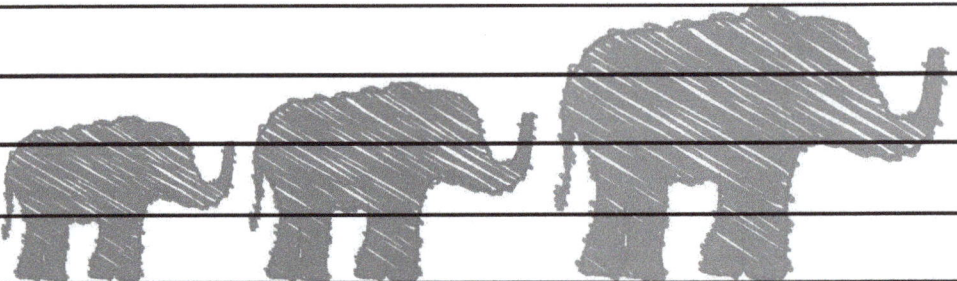

Elder 3:_____

Elder 4:_____

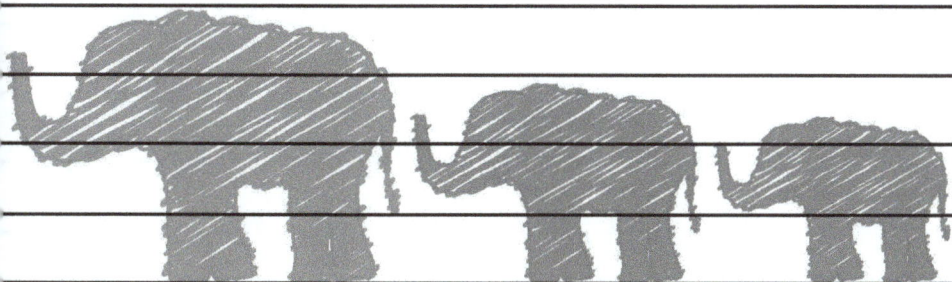

What was it like living with your siblings or being an only child?

Elder 1: _____

_____
_____
_____
_____
_____
_____
_____
_____

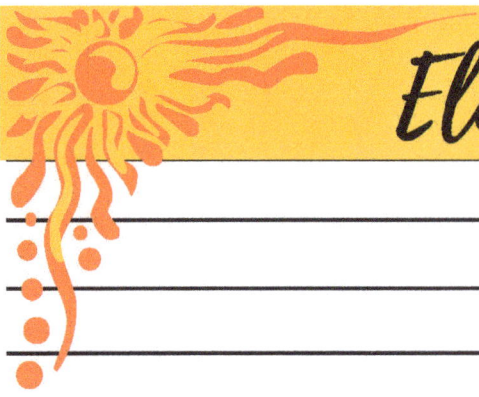

Elder 2 _____

_____
_____
_____
_____

_____
_____

Elder 3:_____

Elder 4:_____

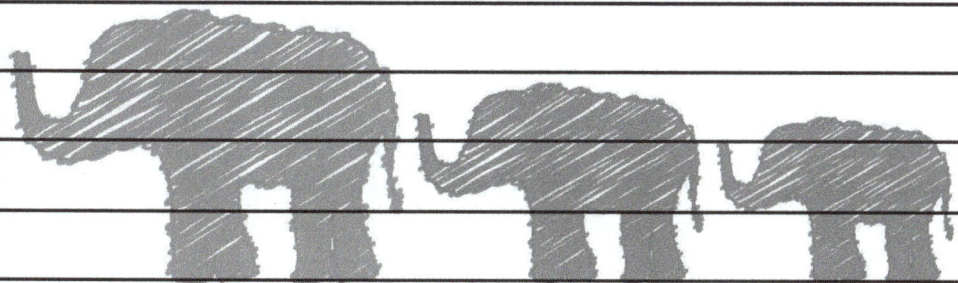

What was it like living with your parents?

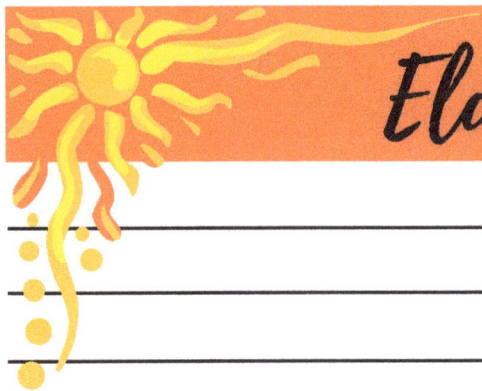

*Elder 1:*_____

_____
_____
_____
_____
_____
_____
_____

*Elder 2*_____

_____
_____
_____
_____

_____
_____

Elder 3:_____

_____
_____
_____
_____
_____
_____
_____
_____
_____

Elder 4:_____

_____
_____
_____
_____
_____
_____
_____

What are some values you have learned that you wish you would implement more?

Elder 1:_____

_____
_____
_____
_____
_____
_____
_____

Elder 2_____

_____
_____
_____

Elder 3:_____

Elder 4:_____

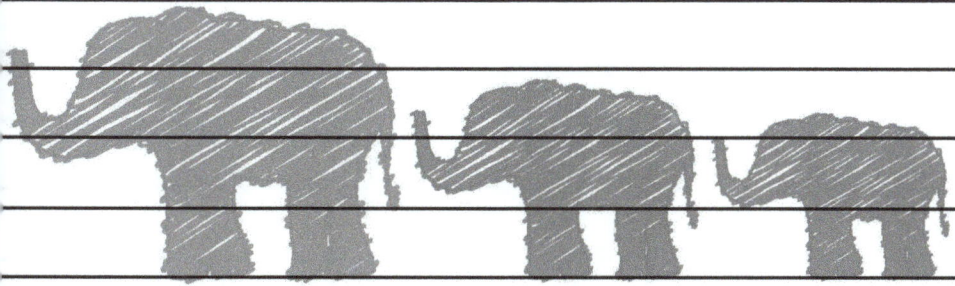

What are some values you have that you wish would be implemented more by others?

*Elder 1:*_____

_____

_____

_____

_____

_____

_____

_____

*Elder 2*_____

_____

_____

_____

_____

_____

Elder 3:_____

Elder 4:_____

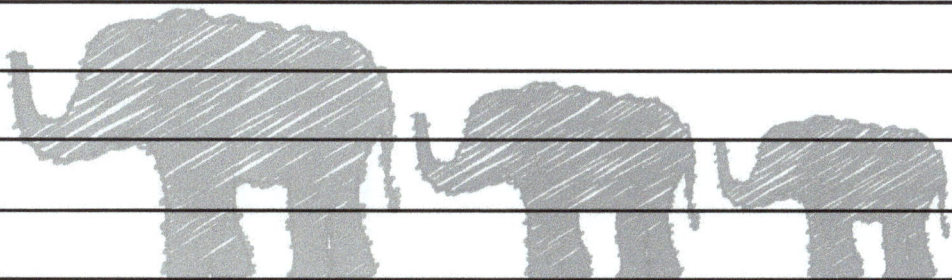

What were your favorite childhood recipes?

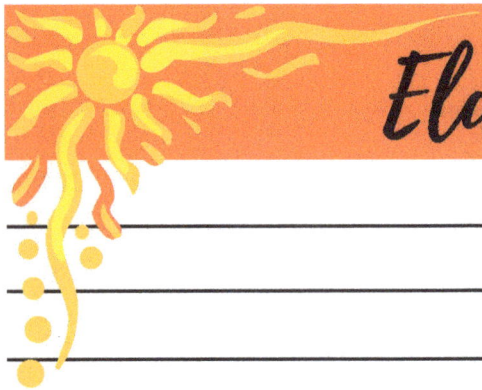

Elder 1:_____

_____
_____
_____
_____
_____
_____
_____
_____
_____

Elder 2_____

_____
_____
_____
_____
_____

Elder 3:_____

Elder 4:_____

What was your favorite song when you were a child?

Elder 1:_____

Elder 2_____

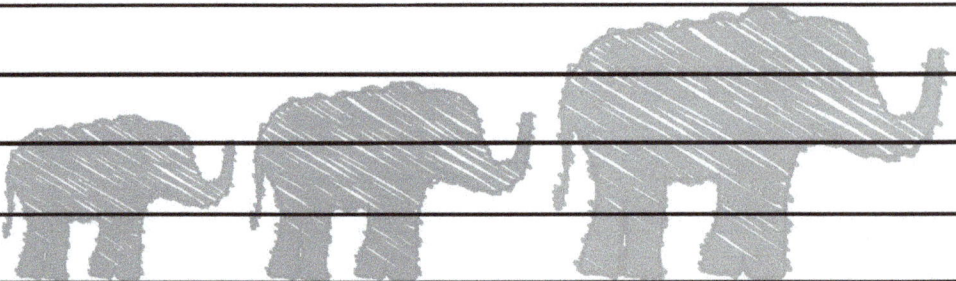

Elder 3:_____

Elder 4:_____

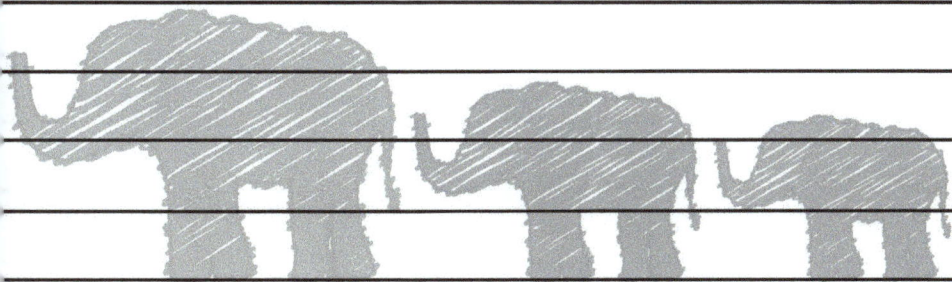

Did you and your family create any traditions?

Elder 1: _____

Elder 2 _____

Elder 3:_____

Elder 4:_____

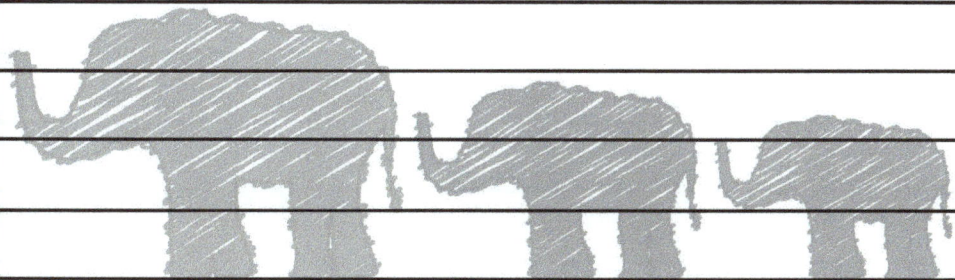

What was your favorite skill or hobby?

Elder 1:_____

_____
_____
_____
_____
_____
_____
_____
_____

Elder 2_____

_____
_____
_____
_____
_____
_____
_____

Elder 3:_____

Elder 4:_____

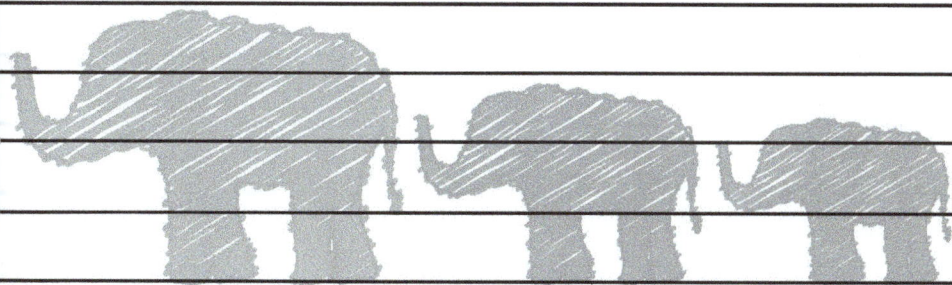

What's one way you'd say you helped change the world?

Elder 1:_____

_____
_____
_____
_____
_____
_____
_____
_____

Elder 2_____

_____
_____
_____
_____
_____

Elder 3:_____

Elder 4:_____

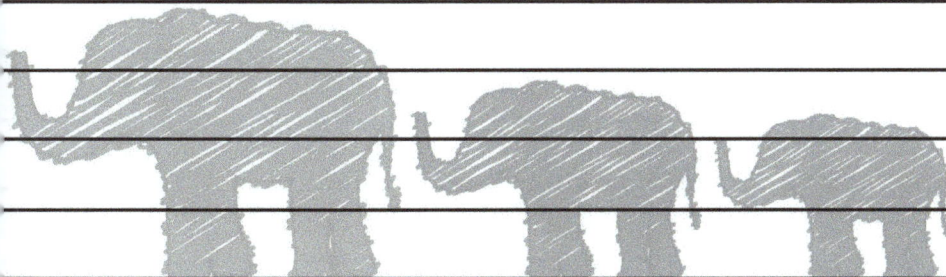

Where was your favorite place to go in your freetime?

*Elder 1:*_____

*Elder 2*_____

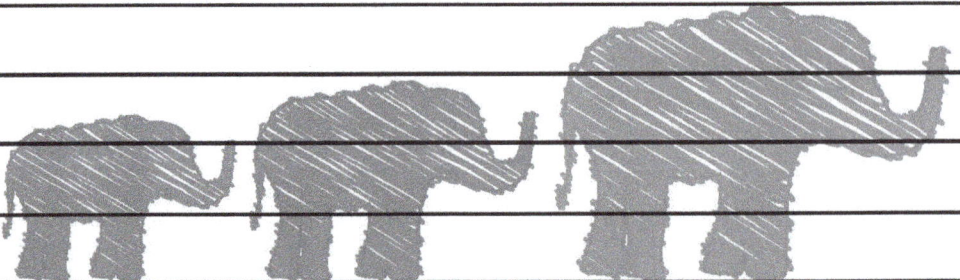

Elder 3:_____

Elder 4:_____

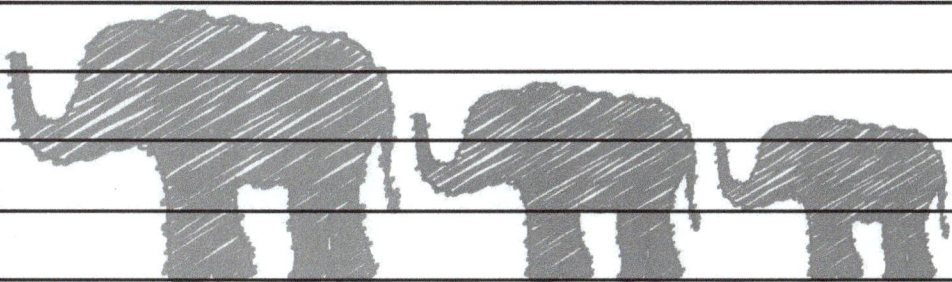

Who was your favorite teacher and why?

Elder 1:_____

_____
_____
_____
_____
_____
_____
_____
_____

Elder 2_____

_____
_____
_____
_____
_____
_____

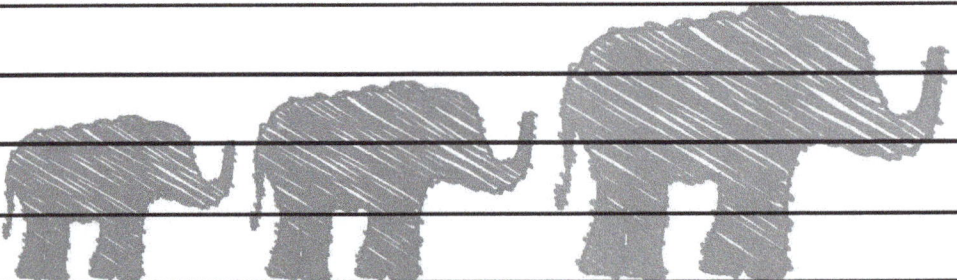

Elder 3:_____

_____
_____
_____
_____
_____
_____
_____
_____
_____
_____
_____

Elder 4:_____

_____
_____
_____
_____
_____
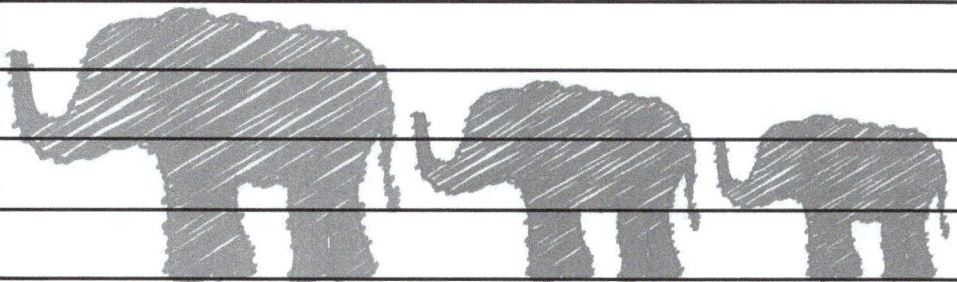
_____
_____

If you could go back to any age, what would it be?

Elder 1:_____

_____

_____

_____

_____

_____

_____

_____

_____

_____

Elder 2_____

_____

_____

_____

_____

_____

Elder 3:_____

Elder 4:_____

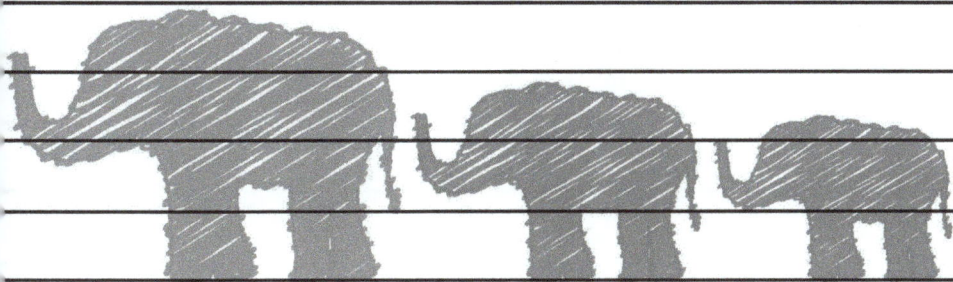

What were your favorite things to do with your friends?

Elder 1:_____

_____
_____
_____
_____
_____
_____
_____
_____

Elder 2_____

_____
_____
_____
_____
_____
_____
_____
_____

Elder 3:_____

Elder 4:_____

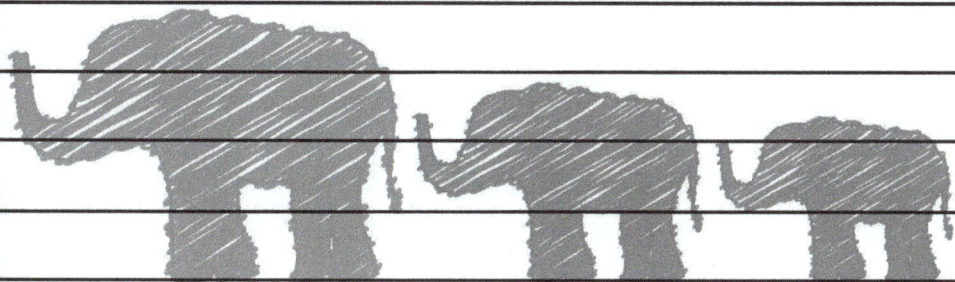

How did you meet your spouse or your first love?

*Elder 1:*_____

_____
_____
_____
_____
_____
_____
_____
_____

*Elder 2*_____

_____
_____
_____
_____
_____
_____

_____

Elder 3:_____

_____
_____
_____
_____
_____
_____
_____
_____
_____
_____
_____

Elder 4:_____

_____
_____
_____
_____
_____
_____
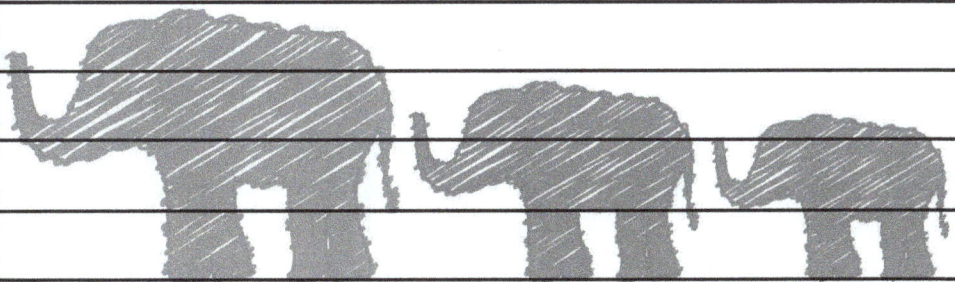

What was your favorite game to play with your family and friends?

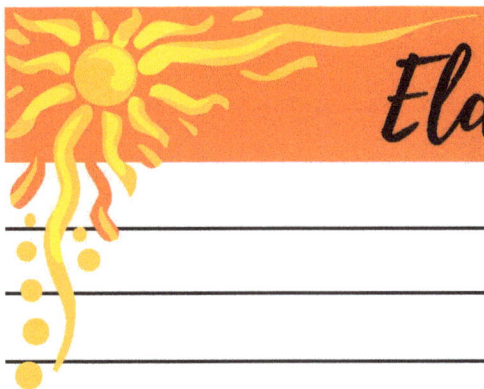

Elder 1:_____

_____
_____
_____
_____
_____
_____
_____
_____

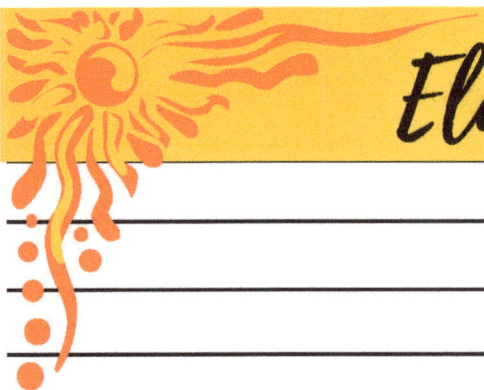

Elder 2_____

_____
_____
_____
_____
_____

Elder 3:_____

Elder 4:_____

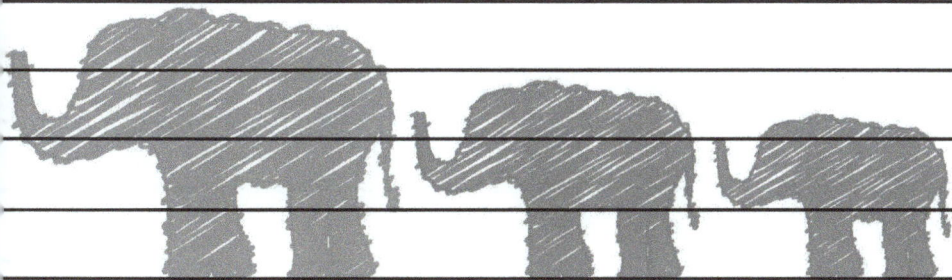

What was the first car you ever drove?

Elder 1:_____

Elder 2_____

Elder 3:_____

Elder 4:_____

What was your favorite vacation and why?

Elder 1:_____

_____
_____
_____
_____
_____
_____
_____

Elder 2_____

_____
_____
_____
_____

Elder 3: _____

Elder 4: _____

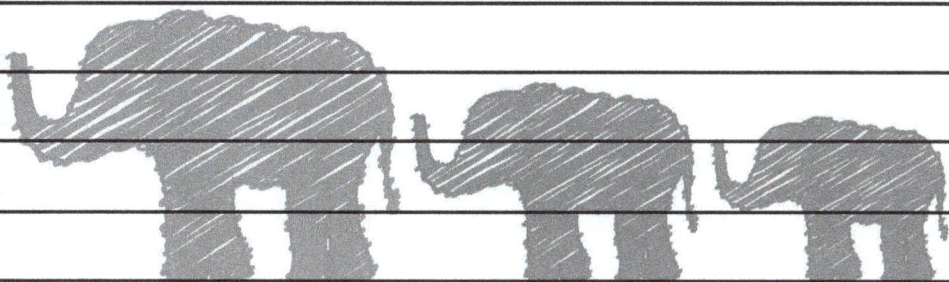

How did you decide what you wanted to be when you grew up?

*Elder 1:*_____

_____
_____
_____
_____
_____
_____
_____
_____

*Elder 2*_____

_____
_____
_____
_____

_____
_____
_____

Elder 3:_____

_____
_____
_____
_____
_____
_____
_____
_____
_____
_____
_____

Elder 4:_____

_____
_____
_____
_____

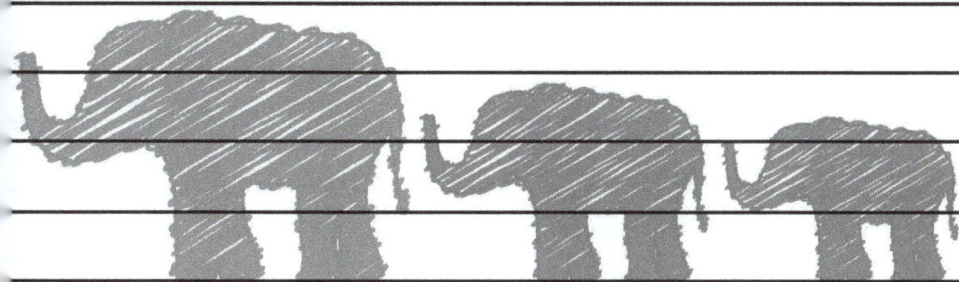

_____
_____
_____
_____

What was a new trend you experienced growing up?

Elder 1:_____

Elder 2_____

Elder 3:_____

Elder 4:_____

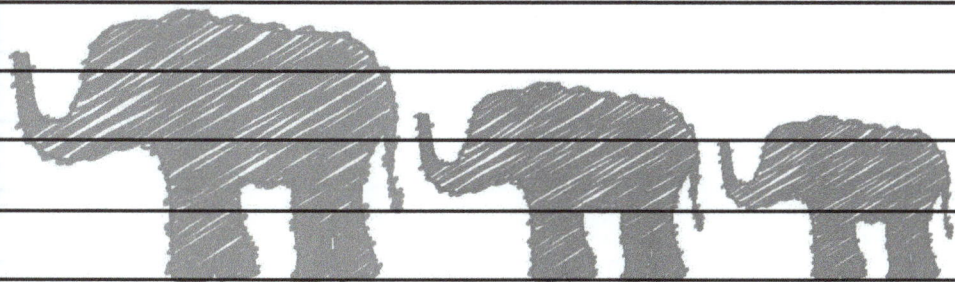

When you were my age, what were you known for?

Elder 1:_____

_____

_____

_____

_____

_____

_____

_____

_____

Elder 2_____

_____

_____

_____

_____

Elder 3:_____

Elder 4:_____

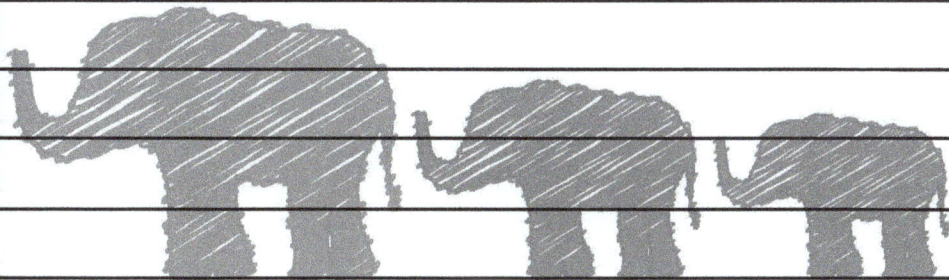

How many times have you moved and how did you feel about it?

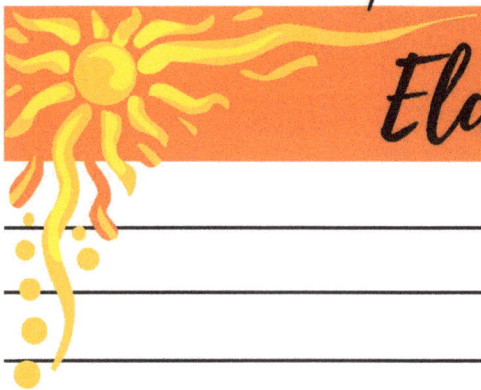

Elder 1:_____

_____

_____

_____

_____

_____

_____

_____

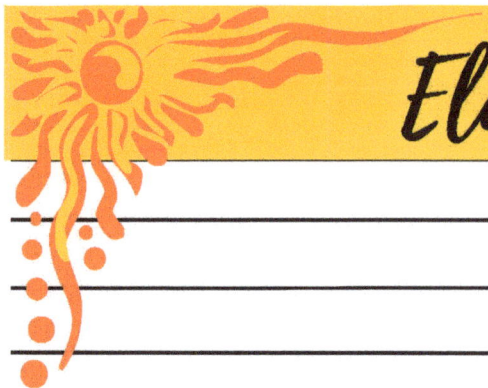

Elder 2_____

_____

_____

_____

_____

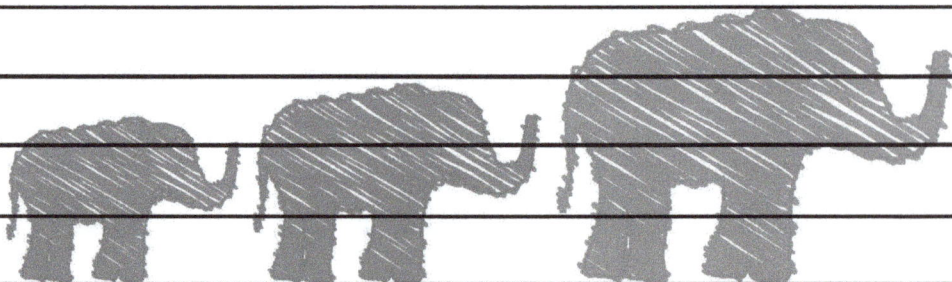

_____

_____

Elder 3:_____

Elder 4:_____

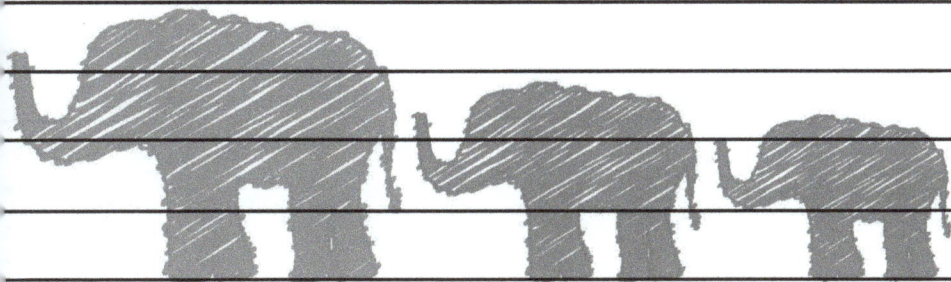

What was the best life lesson your parents or grandparents ever taught you?

Elder 1:_____

Elder 2_____

Elder 3:_____

Elder 4:_____

What is something you are proud of accomplishing in your lifetime?

Elder 1:_____

_____
_____
_____
_____
_____
_____
_____
_____

Elder 2_____

_____
_____
_____
_____
_____

Elder 3:_____

_____
_____
_____
_____
_____
_____
_____
_____
_____
_____

Elder 4:_____

_____
_____
_____
_____

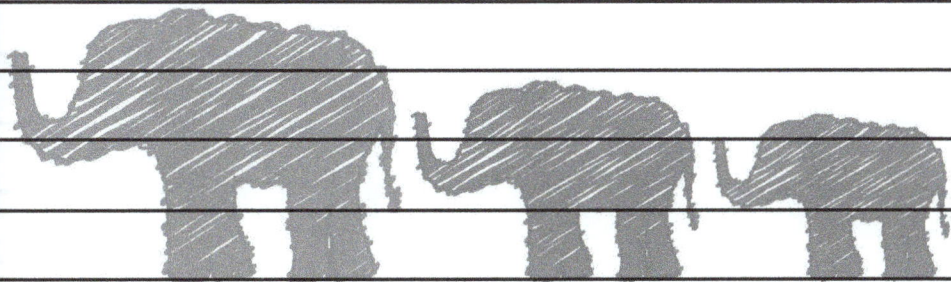

What was your first job?

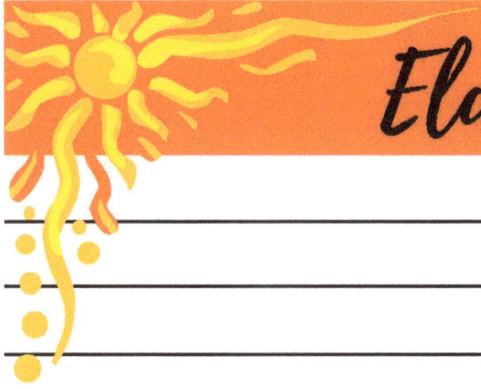

Elder 1:_____

_____

_____

_____

_____

_____

_____

_____

_____

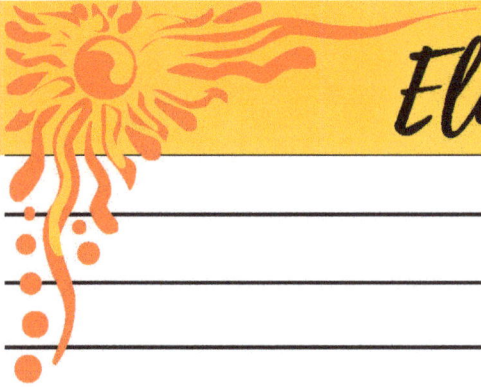

Elder 2_____

_____

_____

_____

_____

_____

_____

_____

Elder 3:_____

Elder 4:_____

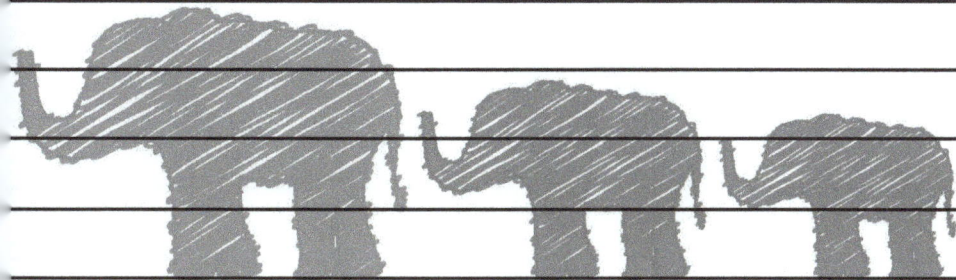

Did you ever have a side hustle? If so, what was it?

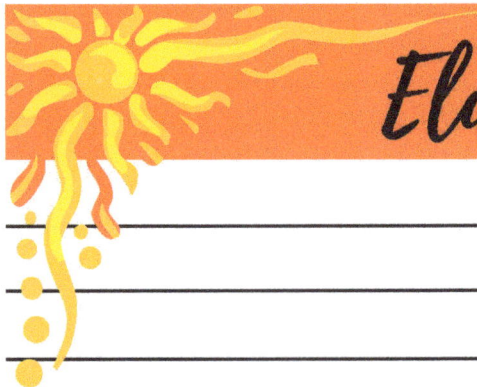

Elder 1:_____

_____

_____

_____

_____

_____

_____

_____

_____

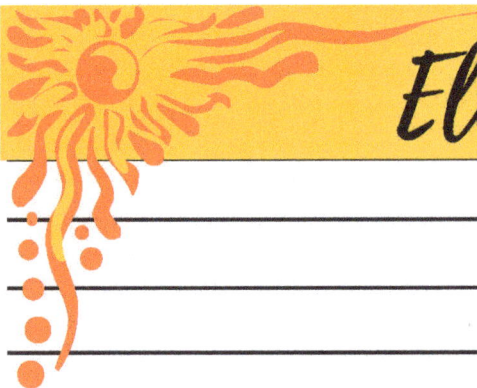

Elder 2_____

_____

_____

_____

_____

_____

_____

_____

Elder 3:_____

_____
_____
_____
_____
_____
_____
_____
_____
_____
_____

Elder 4:_____

_____
_____
_____
_____
_____

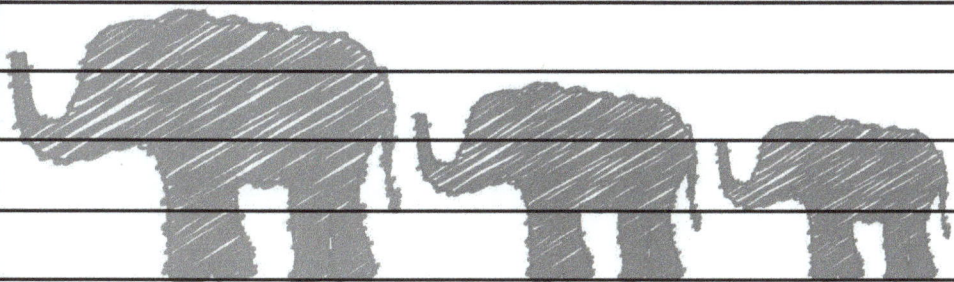

_____
_____
_____

What was a trick or skill you had that nobody you knew could do?

Elder 1:_____

_____
_____
_____
_____
_____
_____
_____
_____

Elder 2_____

_____
_____
_____
_____

_____

Elder 3:_____

_____
_____
_____
_____
_____
_____
_____
_____
_____
_____

Elder 4:_____

_____
_____
_____
_____
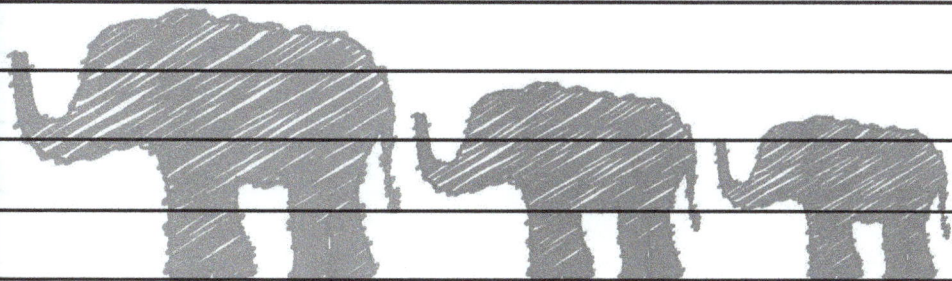

Tell me the names of your best dance moves? Can you teach me how to do one?

Elder 1:_____

Elder 2_____

Elder 3:_____

Elder 4:_____

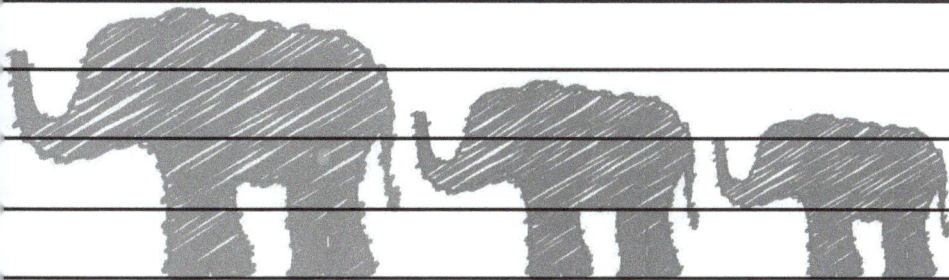

What was the trendy thing to wear when you were my age?

Elder 1:_____

Elder 2_____

Elder 3:_____

Elder 4:_____

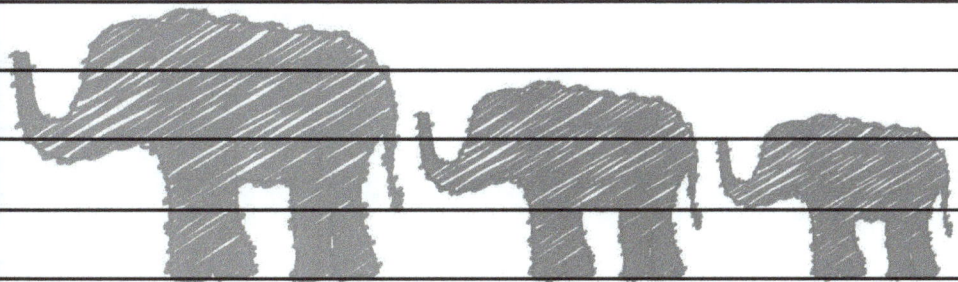

What were some of your favorite books growing up?

Elder 1:_____

Elder 2_____

Elder 3:_____

Elder 4:_____

Free Write

Now that you are moving along with your conversations, you may have thought of other things you want to know.

Use the following pages to ask more questions and to learn more!

Question 1 _____

_____

Elder 1:_____

Elder 2_____

Elder 3:_____

_____
_____
_____
_____
_____
_____
_____
_____
_____

Elder 4:_____

_____
_____
_____
_____
_____
_____
_____
_____

Question 2 _____

_____

Elder 1:_____

Elder 2_____

Elder 3:_____

Elder 4:_____

Question 3 _____

_____

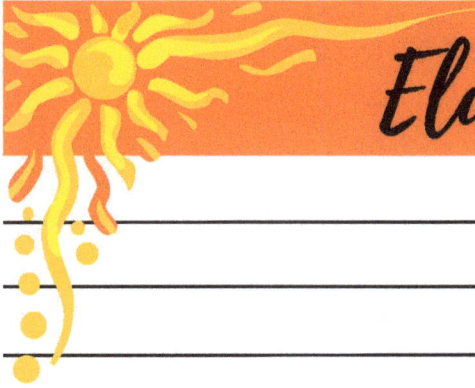

Elder 1:_____

_____

_____

_____

_____

_____

_____

_____

_____

Elder 2_____

_____

_____

_____

_____

_____

_____

Elder 3:_____

Elder 4:_____

Question 4 _____
_____

*Elder 1:*_____

*Elder 2*_____

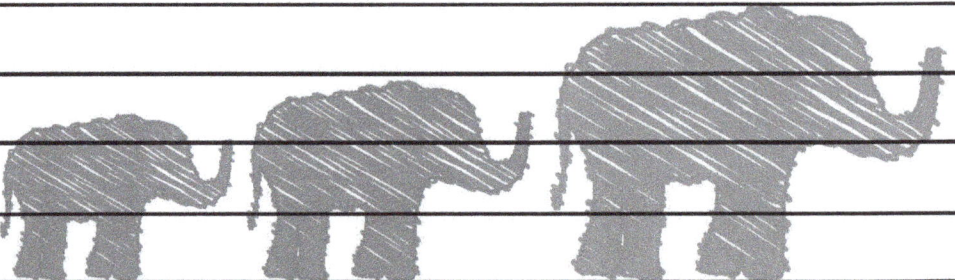

Elder 3:_____

Elder 4:_____

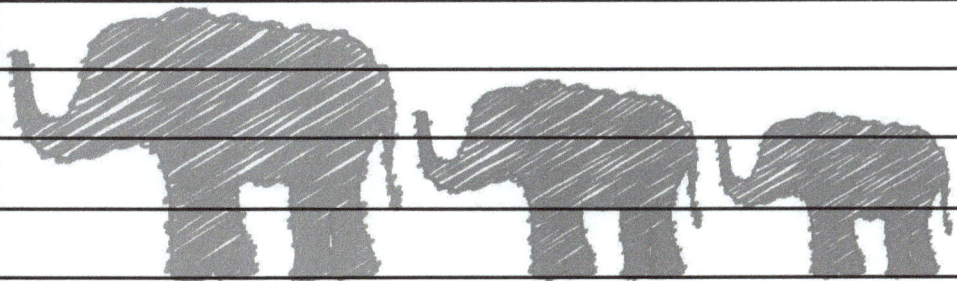

Question 5 _____
_____

 **Elder 1:** _____

Elder 2 _____

Elder 3:_____

Elder 4:_____

Question 6 _____
_____

Elder 1:_____

Elder 2_____

Elder 3: _____

Elder 4: _____

Question 7 _____
_____

Elder 1:_____

Elder 2_____

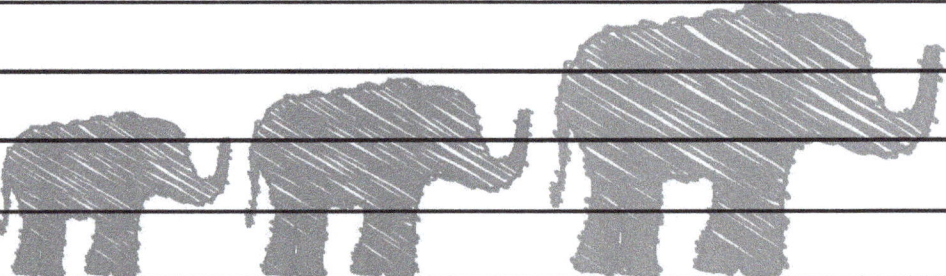

Elder 3:_____

Elder 4:_____

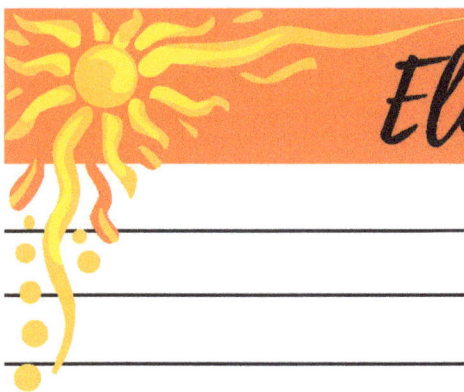

Elder 1:_____

_____
_____
_____
_____
_____
_____
_____
_____
_____

Elder 2_____

_____
_____
_____
_____

_____
_____

Elder 3:_____

_____
_____
_____
_____
_____
_____
_____
_____
_____
_____

Elder 4:_____

_____
_____
_____
_____
_____

Question 9 _____
_____

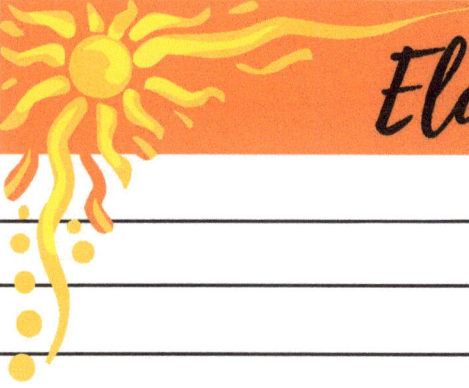

Elder 1:_____

_____
_____
_____
_____
_____
_____
_____

Elder 2_____

_____
_____
_____
_____

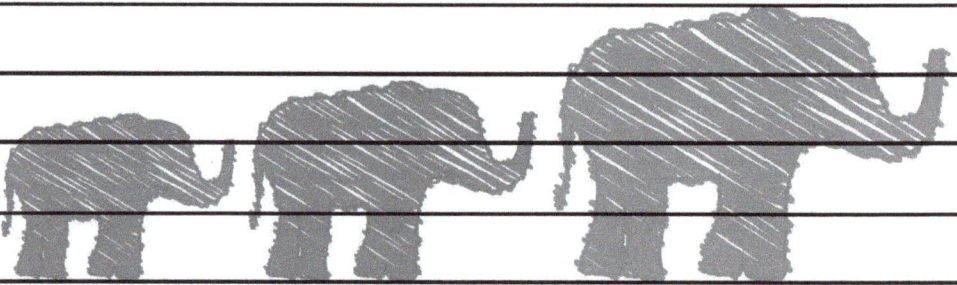

_____
_____
_____

Elder 3:_____

_____
_____
_____
_____
_____
_____
_____
_____
_____
_____

Elder 4:_____

_____
_____
_____
_____
_____

Question 10 _____
_____

Elder 1:_____

_____
_____
_____
_____
_____
_____
_____
_____

Elder 2_____

_____
_____
_____
_____
_____

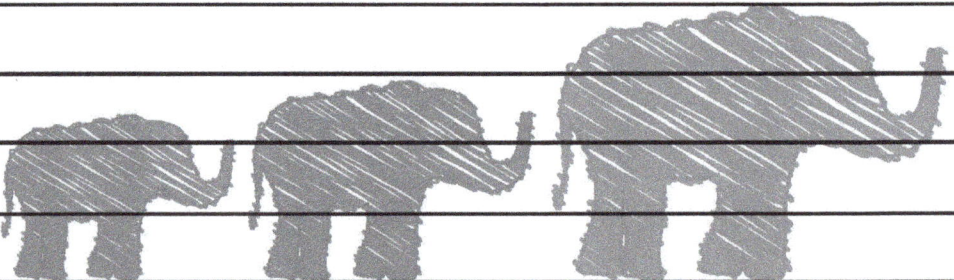

_____
_____
_____
_____

Elder 3:_____

Elder 4:_____